# Utah Bucket List Adventure Guide & Journal

*Explore 50 Natural Wonders You Must See!*

*Bridge Press*

**Bridge Press**
dp@purplelink.org

**Please consider writing a review!**
Just visit: purplelink.org/review

ISBN: 978-1-955149-17-4

# FREE BONUS

Find Out 31 Incredible Places You Can Visit
Next! Just Go To:

**purplelink.org/travel**

# Table of Contents:

# How to Use This Book

Welcome to your very own adventure guide to exploring the natural wonders of the state of Utah. Not only does this book layout the most wonderful places to visit and sights to see in the vast state; it also serves as a journal so that you can record your experience.

**Adventure Guide**
Sorted by region, this guide highlights 50 amazing wonders of nature found in Utah for you to go see and explore. These can be visited in any order, and this book will help keep track of where you've been and where to look forward to going next.

Each portion describes the area or place, what to look for, how to get there, and what you may need to bring along. A map is also included so that you can plot your destinations.

**Document Your Experiences**
There is a blank journal page after the description of each location to help you record your experiences. During or after your visit, you can jot down significant sights you encountered, events that occurred, people involved, and memories you gained while on your adventure. This will add even more value to your experience and keep a record of your time spent witnessing the greatest wonders of Utah.

**GPS Coordinates and Codes**
As you can imagine, not all of the locations in this book have a physical address. Fortunately, some of our listed wonders are either located within a national park or reserve or are near a city, town, or place of business. For those that are not associated with a specific location, it is easiest to map it using GPS coordinates.

Luckily, Google has a system of codes that converts the coordinates into pin-drop locations that Google Maps is able to interpret and navigate.

Each adventure in this guide will include GPS coordinates, general directions on how to find the location, and Google Plus codes whenever possible.

**How to find a location using Google Plus:**

1. Open Google Maps on your device.
2. In the search bar, type the Google Plus code as it is printed on the page.
3. Once the pin is located, you can tap on "Directions" for step-by-step navigation.

It is important that you are prepared for poor cell signals. It's a good practice to route your location and ensure that the directions are accessible offline. Depending on your device and the distance of some locations, you may need to travel with a backup battery source.

# About Utah

Utah became the 45th American state on January 4, 1896. The state's name is derived from the Ute tribe, which means "people of the mountains." Indigenous people have lived in the area for centuries, with archaeological evidence dating back 10,000 years.

Because the land that is now Utah was once a swamp full of dinosaurs, it is one of the best states to find dinosaur fossils. At over 23 feet long, the world's largest raptor lived in Utah and became known as the "Utahraptor."

Encompassing 84,900 square miles, Utah is the 11th largest state in the U.S. in terms of land. It is also one of the "Four Corners" states, along with Arizona, Colorado, and New Mexico. Together, these four states meet at a single point, the only place this occurs in the entire country.

Utah is also a cultural center for Mormonism, with Mormons accounting for around 60% of the state's population. Before it was named Utah, the region was known as "State of Deseret," which means *honey* in the Book of Mormon. The Beehive State's motto is "industry" because of the industrious nature of the honeybee.

This symbol and motto are included on the state flag of Utah. Utahns identify with this imagery because it is hard work to settle in the desert. Major industries such as coal mining, salt production, cattle ranching, and government services are a part of Utah's growing economy.

Utah is also home to five national parks, seven national monuments, and two National Recreation Areas. It is a gorgeous state full of magnificent landscapes to explore and enjoy year-round recreational activities.

# Landscape and Climate

Most of Utah's landscape consists of mountains, high plateaus, and deserts. The state is host to parts of three major geographical areas: the Rocky Mountains, the Basin and Ridge Region, and the Colorado Plateau. On average, the peaks in Utah are the tallest in the country, with King's Peak at the highest point of 13,528 feet.

There are also miles of salt flats as far as the eye can see. These vast areas make it possible to race cars at record-breaking speeds. Drivers can speed for miles without worrying about any obstacles. However, years of this activity have thinned the salt crust substantially.

The western part of the state is a mostly arid desert with small mountain ranges and rugged terrain, while the southern landscape features mesmerizing canyons, mesas, arches, buttes, and gullies. Eastern Utah is full of high-elevation basins and plateaus. The Great Salt Lake is in northern Utah. It's the largest saltwater lake in the Western Hemisphere.

Utah is one of the driest states with low humidity percentages, second only to Nevada. On average, Utah enjoys 300 sunny days per year. The summers are long and scorching hot, and average high temperatures range from 85°F to 100°F in July. Temperatures drop dramatically at night, however, and are cool and pleasant. Winters are short and cold. At the peak of the cold season, temperatures are between 30°F to 55°F.

The mountains near Salt Lake City receive an average of 500 inches of snow per year, which makes for some of the best skiing conditions in the country. In fact, Utah's license plate claims that the state has "the greatest snow on Earth." This is attributed to not only the amount but also the perfect balance of wetness versus fluffiness with a snow density of 8.5%.

# Map of Utah

# Bear Lake

Formed 28,000 years ago by earthquake activity, Bear Lake is 20 miles long, eight miles wide, and 208 feet deep. It is full of natural fresh water and split equally between the states Utah and Idaho at an elevation of 5,924 feet. The lake has been nicknamed the "Caribbean of the Rockies" for the beautiful turquoise color caused by the calcium carbonate suspended in the lake's waters.

Fishing, swimming, skiing, camping, and hiking are popular activities in the area, depending on the season. The lake sits in the middle of the valley, surrounded by mountains. It includes the State Marina and Rendezvous Beach on Utah's side. The park's East Side area consists of Cisco Beach, South Eden, North Eden, Rainbow Cove, and First Point.

**Best time to visit:**
Any time of year, depending on recreational interests.

**Pass/Permit/Fees:**
$15 per day per vehicle, $20 on Saturdays and holidays from June through Labor Day.

**Closest city or town:**
Garden City

**How to get there:**
Take I-15 to US 89/91 in Brigham City. Follow US 89 to Garden City. Turn left on US 89 and travel north one mile before arriving at the park offices.

**GPS coordinates:**
42.0299° N, 111.3322° W

**Did you know?**
The area is regionally famous for its delicious raspberries and raspberry milkshakes.

**Journal:**

Date(s) Visited:

Weather conditions:

Who you were with:

Nature observations:

Special memories:

# Waterfall Canyon

Located just above the city of Ogden, Waterfall Canyon is home to a 300-foot waterfall cascade found at the upper end of the canyon.

The Waterfall Canyon trail is 2.4 miles in and out and is accessible all year round. The steep, rocky hike is worth it for the view of the waterfall and the valley. There are several trails to explore that are clearly marked, but be aware that the trails are surrounded by private property.

The main trail starts off at a large parking lot that is next to a residential tower. There are several trails branching out from this area, so ensure you follow the Bonneville Shoreline Trail (BST).

**Best time to visit:**
Early spring or late fall to avoid crowds.

**Pass/Permit/Fees:**
Free

**Closest city or town:**
Ogden, UT

**How to get there:**
There are multiple trailheads, with the most common located at the top of 29th Street on the east side of Ogden. Follow the trail for Malan Falls as it climbs uphill to the Bonneville Shoreline Trail, then continue to the mouth of Waterfall Canyon. Stay on the main trail from there to the waterfall.

**GPS coordinates:**
Trailhead: 41° 12.637'N, 111° 55.917'W

**Did you know?**
Malan Falls is the unofficial name of the waterfall, named for the family that used to own the land in the area.

**Journal:**

Date(s) Visited:

Weather conditions:

Who you were with:

Nature observations:

Special memories:

# Bonneville Salt Flats

Located in northwestern Utah, the densely packed salt pan named the Bonneville Salt Flats is one of the most unique natural features of the state. Stretching over 30,000 acres, the salt flats were formed when the ancient Lake Bonneville dried up.

A variety of environments exists around the flats depending on the salt levels. The famous Bonneville Speedway is in the western portion. It looks like a frozen lakebed covered with snow. Other areas of the flats feature low mountains and hills, where vegetation is sparse.

An impressive spot to view the Salt Flats is at an established rest stop along I-80. Views of the mountains to the north and west break up the land, while looking to the east and south makes it seem like the flat land extends forever.

**Best time to visit:**
Summer and fall for dry conditions.

**Pass/Permit/Fees:**
Free

**Closest city or town:**
Wendover

**How to get there:**
Take exit 4 off of I-80. Head north and follow signs to the Bonneville Speedway. Take a right onto Leppy Pass Road towards the flats. The parking area is at the end of the road.

**GPS coordinates:**
40.7787° N, 113.8352° W

**Did you know?** Lake Bonneville formed during the late Ice Age and covered nearly two-thirds of Utah.

**Journal:**

Date(s) Visited:

Weather
conditions:

Who you were with:

Nature observations:

Special memories:

# *Uinta Mountains and Mirror Lake Highway*

This part of Utah is popular for fishing, hiking, horseback riding, backpacking, and other outdoor activities. Designated as a roadless wilderness, much of the area prohibits vehicles. Much of the high, pristine mountain range is contained within Ashley National Forest. There is a famous scenic drive that is considered among the most beautiful in the country.

State Route 150, also known as Mirror Lake Scenic Byway, stretches over 70 miles and passes the picturesque Mirror Lake as it traverses into the Uinta Mountains. Scenic viewpoints and numerous campgrounds line this high mountain road. The byway reaches an elevation of 10,687 feet at Bald Mountain Pass.

**Best time to visit:**
June–early October, unless snowmobiling.

**Pass/Permit/Fees:**
A recreation pass is $6 for three days or $12 for seven days.

**Closest city or town:**
Kamas

**How to get there:**
In Kamas, head north on US 189. Turn right onto UT-32. Turn left at State Road to stay on UT-32 and continue until E. Center St/UT-150. Follow UT-150 into the Uinta Mountains. The highway will take you to the Utah–Wyoming state border.

**GPS coordinates:**
40.8827° N, 109.2971° W

**Did you know?**
The Uinta Mountain Range is an east-west chain of mountains.

**Journal:**

Date(s) Visited:

Weather conditions:

Who you were with:

Nature observations:

Special memories:

# The Canyons Near Salt Lake City

Salt Lake City is surrounded by mountains that are bisected by steep canyons. Parleys Canyon, on the east side of the valley, is the most traveled due to I-80. Millcreek Canyon offers extensive hiking trails and is a popular spot for snowshoeing and cross-country skiing in the winter. There are several ski resorts throughout the area.

Hogle Zoo is at the mouth of Emigration Canyon by This is the Place Heritage Park. Butterfield Canyon is southwest of Salt Lake City. It's a popular spot for biking, hiking, and horseback riding. Nearby Bingham Canyon leads to the world's largest open-pit copper mines.

You can visit all seven canyons in any order, and information for Big Cottonwood Canyon is below to help you get started.

**Best time to visit:**
September–November

**Pass/Permit/Fees:**
Free

**Closest city or town:**
Salt Lake City

**How to get there:**
From I-215, head east from the 6200 South exit (exit 6) and follow the signs to Brighton and Solitude ski areas. Turn off of Wasatch Blvd and drive 14.2 miles until you reach Brighton Ski Resort. Drive straight through to the top of the canyon or stop along the way to see the sites.

**GPS coordinates:**
40.6373° N, 111.6330° W

**Did you know?**
The area surrounding Salt Lake City was once covered by the ancient Lake Bonneville.

**Journal:**

Date(s) Visited:

Weather conditions:

Who you were with:

Nature observations:

Special memories:

# Bryce Canyon National Park

Famous for its unique geology, Bryce Canyon features colorful limestone rocks in red, orange, and white. The park contains thousands of spire-shaped rock formations called *hoodoos* that can reach up to 200 feet high.

The expansive Bryce Amphitheater is 12 miles long, three miles wide, and 800 feet deep. It is a part of a series of amphitheaters that extend more than 20 miles within the park. The Rim Trail is the most traveled, but there are other branching trails along the way to explore.

Visitors can also drive through and stop at notable overlooks like Sunrise Point, Sunset Point, Bryce Point, and Inspiration Point. Hiking is always an option, with snowshoeing or skiing in the winter. There are trails for every skill level. Horseback riding and camping are also available. The park is designated as an International Dark Sky Park.

**Best time to visit:**
May–September

**Pass/Permit/Fees:**
$35/vehicle, $30/motorcycle, $20/person. Good for seven days.

**Closest city or town:**
Bryce

**How to get there:**
Take I-15 S to UT-20 E and US 89 S. Exit onto UT-12 E and continue onto UT-63 S. The visitor center is 1 mile inside the park boundary.

**GPS coordinates:**
37.5930° N, 112.1871° W

**Did you know?**
There is a hoodoo in Bryce Canyon National Park called Thor's Hammer because of its unique shape.

**Journal:**

Date(s) Visited:

Weather
conditions:

Who you were with:

Nature observations:

Special memories:

# *Flaming Gorge Reservoir*

Surrounded by the beautiful red-rock mountains, this 91-mile-long reservoir was formed by damming the Green River. Featuring outstanding opportunities for water sports like boating, fishing, parasailing, rafting, or jet skiing, the Flaming Gorge Reservoir is shared between southwest Wyoming and northeastern Utah.

There are three full-service marinas for launching, storing, and maintaining your vessels. At an elevation of 6,040 feet, the temperatures are moderate at around 80°F during the summer months. The reservoir provides an excellent habitat for fish and is famous for its trophy lake fish.

**Best time to visit:**
Spring or summer

**Pass/Permit/Fees:**
No entry fee. A Recreation Use Pass is required at all major boat launches and the Little National Recreation Trail below the dam. It costs $5 per day, $15 for sixteen days, or $35 for an annual pass.

**Closest city or town:**
Manila, UT

**How to get there:**
Highways 191 and 44 are designated as the Flaming Gorge-Uintas National Scenic Byway. At the junction of these two highways, take the HWY 191 fork to the right to drop down to the reservoir.

**GPS coordinates:**
41.0917° N, 109.5390° W

**Did you know?**
The name Flaming Gorge was inspired by the sun reflecting off the bright red rocks around the Green and Colorado rivers.

**Journal:**

Date(s) Visited:

Weather
conditions:

Who you were with:

Nature observations:

Special memories:

# Calf Creek Falls

The Grand Staircase-Escalante National Monument is protected land in southern Utah that holds historical and scientific significance. A perennial stream called Calf Creek is located within the area. There are also two waterfalls that you can visit for a desert oasis experience.

The upper falls are 88 feet high and require a very steep trail to access. The trail is difficult to navigate in some areas, so most people opt for the easier route to the lower falls.

The lower falls hike has a bigger drop and is the more popular of the two. It is a six-mile roundtrip hike that is relatively flat. The waterfall is 126 feet and streams down along the mineral-stained sandstone. A pool at the base is great for swimming and cooling off in the summer.

**Best time to visit:**
Spring–fall, mid-week to avoid crowds.

**Pass/Permit/Fees:**
$5 per vehicle.

**Closest city or town:**
Boulder

**How to get there:**
The trailhead for the lower falls is located at the Calf Creek Campground on Highway 12, 11 miles south of Boulder and 15 miles east of Escalante. The trailhead for the upper falls is located at the south end of Hogback on Highway 12, below Boulder.

**GPS coordinates:**
37.8292° N, 111.4201° W

**Did you know?**
The creek was used as a natural pen for calves in the late 1800s and early 1900s.

**Journal:**

Date(s) Visited:

Weather conditions:

Who you were with:

Nature observations:

Special memories:

# Mystic Hot Springs

Formerly known as Monroe Hot Springs, this location boasts that it's "the best hippie hot springs in the West." The pure mineral water provides a spectacular soaking experience and is naturally heated by the Earth. The spring water emerges from the ground at 168°F and cools to around 100°F as it flows to the smaller pools.

With two concrete pools and six vintage cast iron tubs to choose from in the secluded area, you can enjoy a breathtaking Utah sunset or the Milky Way after dark. There is also an acoustic concert venue to enjoy live music while you relax in the warmth of the water.

**Best time to visit:**
Open all year, less crowded in early spring and fall.

**Pass/Permit/Fees:**
Adult soaking pass: $25. Reservation only. Good for a two-hour time slot.

**Closest city or town:**
Monroe

**How to get there:**
Drive south on I-15 and take exit 188 for Highway 50. Turn right onto Highway 260 towards Aurora, then get onto I-70. Turn left on W. 1300 St., then right onto Highway 118. Once in Monroe, turn left on E. 100 N and go to the end of the road.

**GPS coordinates:**
38.6343° N, 112.1090° W

**Did you know?**
Water from the hot springs carries calcium carbonate, magnesium, and iron.

**Journal:**

Date(s) Visited:

Weather conditions:

Who you were with:

Nature observations:

Special memories:

# Goblin Valley State Park

A showcase of geologic history that started around 170 million years ago, this park was once a vast sea. The inland sea deposited layers of sand, mud, and silt that were sculpted by erosion and wind over time.

The park features hundreds of hoodoos, which are formations of mushroom-shaped pinnacles made from rock. These hoodoos are locally referred to as "goblins," and the otherworldly landscape is often compared to the surface of the planet Mars. The area is surrounded by a wall of eroded cliffs to complete the colorful landscape.

You can do some sightseeing from the park overlook and hike among the fun-shaped goblins on and off-trail. Visitors come to explore, take photos, and view the wildlife.

**Best time to visit:**
Spring and fall

**Pass/Permit/Fees:**
$13 per vehicle per day.

**Closest city or town:**
Green River

**How to get there:**
From I-70, exit onto Highway 24 and drive south for 24 miles to the signed park turnoff. From there, follow the paved road to the park for about 12 miles.

**GPS coordinates:**
38.5737° N, 110.7071° W

**Did you know?**
The movie *Galaxy Quest* was filmed at Goblin Valley.

**Journal:**

Date(s) Visited:

Weather
conditions:

Who you were with:

Nature observations:

Special memories:

# Reflection Canyon

Reflection Canyon is a part of the Glen Canyon National Recreation Area and has a stunning view. The 16–18-mile roundtrip trail is recommended only for experienced adventurers due to its length, terrain, and difficulty to locate. The view is in a remote location and can be done in a one-day hiking trip; however, some opt to backpack overnight to rise with the sun.

You will need a vehicle with a high profile and four-wheel drive to access the trailhead via an unmaintained and unpaved route. There is no clearly marked trail, so prepare to navigate carefully.

**Best time to visit:**
March–November

**Pass/Permit/Fees:**
$30 per vehicle, $25 per motorcycle, $15 on foot or by bicycle. Backcountry permit required for all overnight trips.

**Closest city or town:**
Kanab

**How to get there:**
Drive 50 miles down Hole-in-the-Rock Road to a small parking area on the right. The canyon is southeast, but you must go southwest first. Face south and keep close to the straight cliff's edge on your right. After five miles, there will be a flat, squared-off face to the cliffs. Turn southeast and keep the cliffs to your back. Continue two miles to the canyon.

**GPS coordinates:**
37.1883° N, 110.9184° W

**Did you know?**
The location of this wonder was revealed in 2006 when photographer Michael Melford's photos of the canyon were published in *National*

**Journal:**

Date(s) Visited:

Weather conditions:

Who you were with:

Nature observations:

Special memories:

# Peekaboo and Spooky Slot Canyon Loop

A family favorite in the Dry Fork area of the Grand Staircase-Escalante area, Spooky Gulch is famous for how dark and narrow it gets inside. Nearby, Peekaboo Gulch is full of beautiful sandstone arches.

These canyons are a scenic vista of red and purple rock, and the natural contours and waves of the sandstone are awe-inspiring. There is some tame climbing and rock scrambling involved, so it is a moderately difficult trek. These adventures can be done individually, but they pair perfectly in a loop that you can tackle in one afternoon.

The recommended route is to take Peekaboo Gulch first, which takes you north. Upon exiting, hike overland to the east for half a mile until you reach Spooky Gulch. The entire loop is about three miles and takes most hikers around three to four hours.

**Best time to visit:**
Spring or fall

**Pass/Permit/Fees:**
Free

**Closest city or town:**
Escalante

**How to get there:**
Take Highway 26 miles to Hole-in-the-Rock Road. Drive 26 miles and then turn onto Dry Fork Road. There is a parking lot at the end that overlooks the rock formations. Climb down from the overlook into the bottom of Dry Fork, and Peekaboo will be ahead, traveling north.

**GPS coordinates:**
37.4814° N, 111.2166° W

**Did you know?**
Spooky Gulch is only ten inches wide in some spots.

28

**Journal:**

Date(s) Visited:

Weather conditions:

Who you were with:

Nature observations:

Special memories:

# Coyote Gulch

Coyote Gulch is a winding, semi-narrow canyon located in the Grand Staircase-Escalante desert. Expect to see arches, wetlands, domes, waterfalls, and a natural bridge set within red rock country.

One of the more popular routes is through Crack-in-the-Rock, but there are several options for accessing the gulch. The "Sneaker Route" is the most direct and can be traveled within a day. The latter requires rope for the descent into the gulch.

At up to 26 miles, the entire canyon adventure is well suited for an overnight camp, especially since you will definitely want to explore as you go. You can customize your route to be shorter as needed. Either way, be prepared for some serious navigation and rock scrambling.

**Best time to visit:**
Spring or fall

**Pass/Permit/Fees:**
No entry fee. Free permit required for camping or backpacking.

**Closest city or town:**
Escalante

**How to get there:**
Drive on Highway 12 until you reach Hole-in-the-Rock Road.

**GPS coordinates:**
37.4279° N, 110.9809° W

**Did you know?**
Stevens Arch is one of the largest arches in the U.S. It can be found northeast of the Escalante-Coyote Gulch confluence.

**Journal:**

Date(s) Visited:

Weather
conditions:

Who you were with:

Nature observations:

Special memories:

# Corona Arch

Corona Arch is a 140-foot-wide natural sandstone arch that curves out from a massive stone mountain. This arch is part of the same rock formation as Pinto Arch and Bowtie Arch, which you will pass along the way.

The Corona Arch Trail is three miles roundtrip, making it a short hike to a spectacular view of the arch. However, this hike is rated as moderately difficult, and safety cables and ladders are involved.

**Best time to visit:**
Fall or spring

**Pass/Permit/Fees:**
Free

**Closest city or town:**
Moab

**How to get there:**
From Moab, drive northwest on US 191. Turn left and go south on UT-279/Potash Rd. Go 10 miles to a sign for the Corona Arch Trailhead on the right side of the road. Follow the trail east and cross the railroad tracks. Continue northeast towards the base of the sandstone cliff, then continue following the base east until you see a safety cable. After traversing the first safety cable, you will see the arch in the distance.

**GPS coordinates:**
38.5799° N, 109.6201° W

**Did you know?** Corona Arch is also known as the "Little Rainbow Bridge" due to its resemblance to the famous Rainbow Bridge.

**Journal:**

Date(s) Visited:

Weather
conditions:


Who you were with:


Nature observations:


Special memories:

# Monument Valley

Located on the Utah–Arizona state border, Monument Valley is known for the towering sandstone buttes in the area. These sandstone masterpieces are found along with colossal mesas and panoramic views in the Monument Valley Navajo Tribal Park. The towers reach heights of 400–1,000 feet, and the landscape is overwhelmingly beautiful.

It is possible to drive through Monument Valley and visit the main sites within a few hours. If you really want to explore, consider spending the day. Tribal Park Loop is a 17-mile scenic drive past the most popular sites.

The only self-guided tour available is the Wildcat Trail, and all other hikes must be done with a guide. There are many options for tours depending on how much time you wish to spend. Valley Drive and Forrest Gump are the must-do activities.

**Best time to visit:**
Spring and fall

**Pass/Permit/Fees:**
$20 per vehicle entry fee. Tours cost around $80–$90 depending on the tour company, with one overnight excursion costing up to $300.

**Closest city or town:**
Mexican Hat

**How to get there:**
Park access is on US 163, just north of the Utah–Arizona border.

**GPS coordinates:**
36.9980° N, 110.0985° W

**Did you know?** This iconic landscape has been featured in many popular movies, including *Forrest Gump, National Lampoon's Journal:*

**Journal:**

Date(s) Visited:

Weather conditions:

Who you were with:

Nature observations:

Special memories:

# Cedar Breaks National Monument

A natural amphitheater with a rim over 10,000 feet above sea level, Cedar Breaks stretches across three miles with a depth of over 2,000 feet. The canyon was formed from erosion and uplift over millions of years. Much of the area at the top is covered in volcanic rock, and the muted rainbow colors offer amazing scenery.

There are a variety of hiking trails to explore, many of which are ranked as easy to moderate. Sunset Trail runs between two overlooks; Nature Trail is great for wildlife viewing. Alpine Pond Loop Trail forms a figure eight through forests and meadows, and South Rim Trail offers spectacular views all around. Trails start at over 10,000 feet in elevation, so it's best to get acclimated first. The steepness of the amphitheater does not allow climbing down from the rim, but you can explore the bottom by starting in Dixie National Forest.

**Best time to visit:**
June–October

**Pass/Permit/Fees:**
$10 entry fee, good for seven days.

**Closest city or town:**
Cedar City

**How to get there:**
Take I-15 north to Cedar City. Exit onto U-14 East from Cedar City and drive to U-148. Turn left to Cedar Breaks.

**GPS coordinates:** 37.6347° N, 112.8451° W

**Did you know?**
The park is situated in one of the largest regions of natural darkness in the lower 48 states, offering opportunities for astrotourism.

**Journal:**

Date(s) Visited:

Weather conditions:

Who you were with:

Nature observations:

Special memories:

# Red Canyon

Called the "most photographed place in Utah," this canyon in the Dixie National Forest is exceptionally scenic with Ponderosa pines set against a background of red sandstone and spires. There are views of hoodoo formations, red cliffs, and pink soil, too.

The trails are extensive and well maintained. Birdseye Trail is a 0.8-mile hike featuring close-up views of the red rock formations. Losee Canyon Trail is three miles and provides a more rugged trek. Casto Canyon trail allows for off-highway vehicle usage, but you should check with the visitor center about off-road trail use.

There is the Red Canyon Travel Kiosk, located just east of the visitor center, where five different trails can be accessed. You will definitely want a map!

**Best time to visit:**
May–September

**Pass/Permit/Fees:**
Free

**Closest city or town:** Panguitch

**How to get there:**
Approximately seven miles from Panguitch on Highway 89, turn east onto Highway 12. From that junction, it is approximately 3.5 miles to the Visitor Center, which is located near the Red Canyon Campground.

**GPS coordinates:**
37.7458° N, 112.3380° W

**Did you know?**
The landscape of Red Canyon is very similar to the famous Bryce Canyon, just on a smaller scale.

**Journal:**

Date(s) Visited:

Weather conditions:

Who you were with:

Nature observations:

Special memories:

# Kanarra Falls

Kanarra Creek offers a slot canyon water hike in a canyon that features waterfalls and a natural water slide. Water flows year-round, so hikers must wade the stream at certain places on the trail. There are two waterfalls, with the first waterfall approximately 1.6 miles into the hike. The hike to the first waterfall is easy and short, but if you want a moderate challenge, you can climb the falls and continue into the canyon.

To continue past the first waterfall, you will need to scale a lean-to log ladder with metal rungs. Further on, you will also need to scale a large boulder with no ladders or handholds. The route and length of this adventure are customizable, so you can choose to keep it easy or go for more of a challenge.

**Best time to visit:**
Do not enter this canyon when flash flood warnings are in effect in the Kanarraville, Cedar Breaks, or Zion areas.

**Pass/Permit/Fees:**
$12 required permit. The hike is limited to 150 people per day.

**Closest city or town:**
Kanrraville

**How to get there:**
Take I-15 and exit at Kanarraville. Drive to the center of town and follow 100 N about four blocks east to the parking lot. Walk up the trail to the gate, where you'll encounter the permit kiosk. Hike up the canyon, staying above the stream when possible.

**GPS coordinates:**
37.5377° N, 113.1525° W

**Did you know?**
These waterfalls are two of the most photographed waterfalls in Utah.

**Journal:**

Date(s) Visited:

Weather conditions:

Who you were with:

Nature observations:

Special memories:

# *Yant Flats*

Not a widely known location, Yant Flats is the southern boundary of a rocky plateau that is richly colored in shades of orange, pink, red, yellow, and white. The Yant Flats trail leads across the southern slopes of the Pine Valley Mountains. It is 3.4 miles roundtrip on a trail that is rated as moderate.

Over time, the sandstone layers at the edge of the Colorado Plateau have been pushed up by an underlying volcanic rock. After being exposed, they've eroded into domes, cliffs, and canyons. The layers of rock and their colors have created an incredible marbled effect with remarkably colored sandstone formations.

**Best time to visit:**
Spring or fall

**Pass/Permit/Fees:**
Free

**Closest city or town:**
Leeds

**How to get there:** The best approach is from the east, beginning at Leeds along I-15. Take exit 22 to Leeds/Silver Reef. Turn left onto Main St. and head north for about 1.5 miles. Turn left onto Silver Reed Road and follow for 1.2 miles until it turns in a dirt road called Oak Grove Road. Continue for two miles. At the fork, keep left for St. George. Follow this road for seven miles until you reach your destination on the left.

**GPS coordinates:**
37.2300° N, 113.4683° W

**Did you know?**
The cliffs in the area are so colorful that they are called the "candy cliffs of Utah."

**Journal:**

Date(s) Visited:

Weather
conditions:

Who you were with:

Nature observations:

Special memories:

# Snow Canyon State Park

A 7,400-acre scenic park located in the Red Cliff Desert Reserve, Snow Canyon State Park is full of strikingly colorful majestic views. The area is surrounded by ancient lava flows and red Navajo sandstone, offering stunning red rock vistas.

The park's distinctive landscapes were shaped by lava flows and sand as recently as 27,000 years ago. You can explore the sandstone cliffs, petrified sand dunes, and lava fields of this terrain.

With more than 38 miles of hiking trails, a three-mile paved trail for walking and biking, and 15 miles of equestrian trails, there are plenty of areas to explore on this adventure.

**Best time to visit:**
Spring and fall

**Pass/Permit/Fees:**
$10 fee per vehicle, $5 per group of pedestrians/cyclists (up to eight people).

**Closest city or town:**
St. George

**How to get there:**
Take I-15 to Snow Canyon Parkway. Proceed approximately 3.5 miles and turn right onto Snow Canyon Drive. Follow this road to enter the park via the south entrance.

**GPS coordinates:**
37.2178° N, 113.6396° W

**Did you know?** Contrary to its name, this park seldom receives snow. It was named after early Utah leaders Lorenzo and Erastus Snow.

**Journal:**

Date(s) Visited:

Weather conditions:

Who you were with:

Nature observations:

Special memories:

# Canyonlands National Park

This dramatic desert landscape was carved by the Colorado River. The park is divided into four regions, and most people focus on one area per visit. There is no bridge or road that connects the districts in the park.

Island in the Sky is the most accessible, boasting a scenic drive featuring views of buttes, canyons, and numerous hikes. Towering rock pinnacles known as the Needles compose the Needles district. This area requires a backcountry approach and involves more strenuous hiking and four-wheel drive.

The most isolated district is The Maze. Its remoteness is best accessed by experienced hikers due to its challenging backpacking, off-roading, and hiking trails. You can also book a river trip up the Green or Colorado rivers and see the area by boat.

**Best time to visit:**
Spring and fall

**Pass/Permit/Fees:**
Private vehicle entry fee: $30, motorcycle: $25, by foot/bicycle: $15.

**Closest city or town:**
Moab

**How to get there:**
From US 191 north of Moab, UT-313 leads to Island in the Sky. From US 191 south of Moab, UT-211 leads to The Needles. Unpaved roads reach The Maze (graded dirt, four-wheel-drive a must) via the Hans Flat Ranger Station. These roads may become impassable when wet.

**GPS coordinates:**
38.2136° N, 109.9025° W

**Did you know?**
This park covers a total area of 337,598 acres.

**Journal:**

Date(s) Visited:

Weather conditions:

Who you were with:

Nature observations:

Special memories:

# *Arches National Park*

Arches National Park has the world's largest concentration of natural sandstone arches. There is also an astounding variety of other geological formations, such as colossal sandstone fins, soaring pinnacles, massive rocks, and spires.

One option to see the park is via the 36-mile roundtrip paved scenic drive that leads visitors to several of the major viewpoints. There is a wide variety of trails, some as short as 20 minutes, and many of them rated easy. You can even combine parts of the scenic drive with specific trails to customize your own adventure.

Many of these trails lead to formations deserving of their own entries found later in our guide, such as Double Arch, Windows Trail, Delicate Arch, and Devil's Garden Trails.

**Best time to visit:**
Spring and fall

**Pass/Permit/Fees:**
$30 per vehicle, $25 per motorcycle, and $15 per individual. Good for seven days.

**Closest city or town:**
Moab

**How to get there:**
The entrance to the park is five miles north of Moab along Highway 191.

**GPS coordinates:**
38.7331° N, 109.5925° W

**Did you know?**
This park is home to more than 2,000 natural sandstone arches.

**Journal:**

Date(s) Visited:

Weather
conditions:

Who you were with:

Nature observations:

Special memories:

# Zion National Park

Zion Canyon offers panoramic views of steep red cliffs made from rock that is around 270 million years old. The photogenic area also contains diverse terrain and hiking options for all skill levels.

Observation Point is an eight-mile trail to a summit offering a spectacular view of nearly every major attraction in the canyon. Angels Landing is strenuous, requiring the use of chains bolted into the cliffs. Emerald Pools is also a favorite, featuring a series of desert oases full of waterfalls, lush vegetation, and red rock monoliths.

You can tour the scenic drive via shuttle bus. It begins President's Day weekend and continues on the weekends until daily service begins in March. Private vehicles aren't permitted when the shuttle is in service.

**Best time to visit:**
Spring and fall

**Pass/Permit/Fees:**
A pass is required. $35 per vehicle, $30 per motorcycle, and $20 for pedestrians, all valid for seven days. Shuttle tickets are $1 and must be purchased online in advance—wilderness permit required for overnight backpacking, canyoneering, climbing, narrows, and subway.

**Closest city or town:**
Springdale

**How to get there:**
Take I-15 S to Exit 27 and follow Route 17 for six miles. Take Route 9 E into the hills. Drive 19 miles to Springdale, the gateway to the park.

**GPS coordinates:**
37.2982° N, 113.0263° W

**Did you know?**
Zion was the first national park in Utah.

**Journal:**

Date(s) Visited:

Weather
conditions:

Who you were with:

Nature observations:

Special memories:

# *Diamond Fork Hot Springs*

The warm, cobalt blue water of the Diamond Fork Hot Springs is both lovely to see and great for a relaxing soak. Several pools are available for soaking with the sounds and views of three lovely waterfalls nearby. The forestry and red cliffs provide the perfect backdrop to the area.

The trail to the hot springs is a little over two miles from the trailhead, with a gradual elevation gain of 700 feet. The first half follows along the left side of Sixth Water Creek, and you will know when you are approaching the hot springs from the smell of the sulfur.

If visiting in the winter, you might need to bring snowshoes if the snow isn't packed down on the trail. There is a road closure due to snow in the winter, so the trek is a bit longer.

**Best time to visit:**
September–early November to avoid crowds.

**Pass/Permit/Fees:**
Free

**Closest city or town:**
Springville

**How to get there:**
From Salt Lake City, head south on 1-15 until you reach the town of Spanish Fork. Take exit 257 onto US 6 E. Drive for 11 miles, then take a left at mile marker 184 onto Diamond Fork Road. Continue 10 miles until you reach the sign for the trailhead parking lot on the right.

**GPS coordinates:**
40.0845° N, 111.3550° W

**Did you know?** Diamond Fork Hot Springs used to be called Fifth Water Hot Springs.

**Journal:**

Date(s) Visited:

Weather conditions:

Who you were with:

Nature observations:

Special memories:

# Baker Hot Springs

Baker Hot Springs is a more rustic, less frequented spring to visit. This desolate location features small natural hot springs surrounded by a vast desert landscape. There are three concrete soaking tubs that can accommodate several people. A neat feature is the trench system, which brings hot water in on one side and cool water from the other side. The cool water is sourced from another natural spring in the area. You can alter the flow of each to control the temperature of the water.

Also known as Crater Springs and Abraham Hot Springs, these springs are accessible by car. Be aware of road conditions because the location is a bit off the beaten path. Camping is permitted in the area.

**Best time to visit:**
Winter, spring, or fall

**Pass/Permit/Fees:**
Free

**Closest city or town:**
Delta

**How to get there:** From downtown Delta, head west on Main St. Go over the bridge and turn right onto 1000 W. Follow for 1.6 miles until it becomes 1500 N. Turn right onto Jones Rd. Continue nine miles and turn left at the junction. Continue 11 miles to Baker Hot Springs Road on the right. Follow the dirt road 7.2 miles to the hot springs on the right.

**GPS coordinates:**
39.6127° N, 112.7291° W

**Did you know?**
The Baker Hot Springs are heated by the volcanic activity of Fumarole Butte.

**Journal:**

Date(s) Visited:

Weather conditions:

Who you were with:

Nature observations:

Special memories:

# Homestead Crater

There is a hidden underground cave about an hour outside of Salt Lake City. The Homestead Crater is a geothermal hot spring located inside a 55-foot dome of limestone. The cave is beehive-shaped with a hole at the top that welcomes sunlight and fresh air. The inside is heated by the springs. The water is consistently 90–96°F.

The spring is 65 feet deep, and 400 feet wide at the base, and its warm temperatures make it a fitting spot for traditional hot spring soaks, scuba diving, snorkeling, and exploring the crater. You can paddleboard through the hot spring. There are paddleboard yoga classes offered too.

**Best time to visit:**
Any time of year

**Pass/Permit/Fees:**
Mon.-Thurs. fees: $13 for swim/soak (40 min.), $18 for snorkeling (40 min.), $22 for a scuba dive (1 hour). Fri.-Sun. fees: $16 for swim/soak (40 min.), $21 for snorkeling (40 min.), $27 for a scuba dive (1 hour).

**Closest city or town:**
Midway

**How to get there:**
From Salt Lake City, take I-80 E approximately 32 miles to US 40 (Heber Exit 146). Travel south 14 miles to the Midway and Wasatch Mountain State Park turnoff. Turn right onto River Rd and follow the road approximately 2.5 miles to the roundabout. Turn right onto Burgi Lane (1050 N). Follow the green signs 2.1 miles to the entrance.

**GPS coordinates:**
40.5239° N, 111.4850° W

**Did you know?**
This crater is the only warm scuba diving destination in the continental U.S.

**Journal:**

Date(s) Visited:

Weather conditions:

Who you were with:

Nature observations:

Special memories:

# *Balanced Rock*

Located right in the middle of Arches National Park, Balanced Rock towers overhead at the height of 128 feet. A large rock balanced on a narrow pedestal of stone, it is one of the most popular sites at the park. It is located near the park's main road, a little over nine miles from the entrance.

There is an easy, short loop trail of about 0.3 miles that takes you around the base of the rock formation. As the forces of nature continue to erode the rock, the large rock will eventually collapse. This is because the large rock that is balancing on the lower rocks is made of harder rock that erodes more slowly.

**Best time to visit:**
Spring or fall

**Pass/Permit/Fees:**
$30 per vehicle, $25 per motorcycle, and $15 per individual. Good for seven days.

**Closest city or town:**
Moab

**How to get there:**
The entrance to the park is five miles north of Moab along Highway 191. From the Visitor Center, continue on the Arches Entrance Road (now called the Arches Scenic Drive) for 8.9 miles to the Balance Rock trailhead located on the right (east) side of the road.

**GPS coordinates:**
38.7010° N, 109.5645° W

**Did you know?**
The rock that is balancing on the upper portion of the formation is as large as three school buses and is presumed to weigh 3,577 tons.

**Journal:**

Date(s) Visited:

Weather conditions:

Who you were with:

Nature observations:

Special memories:

# Windows Trail

Windows Trail is a leisurely trail in Arches National Park that can take you to other parts of the area. This easy trail is about a mile long and visits three impressive arches along the way.

The main attraction is the two arches standing side by side, separated by some distance. They're known as the North Window and South Window. These two arches are cut from the same sandstone fin, with a gigantic fin remnant of over 100 feet wide between them. The Turret Arch is southwest of these "windows." It sits within a tower-like rock formation. The entire area is full of captivating stone formations.

**Best time to visit:**
Spring or fall

**Pass/Permit/Fees:**
$30 per vehicle, $25 per motorcycle, and $15 per individual. Good for seven days.

**Closest city or town:**
Moab

**How to get there:**
The entrance to the park is five miles north of Moab along Highway 191. Drive 9.2 miles up the Arches Entrance Road/Arches Scenic Drive, then take the first right after Balanced Rock. Continue to follow this road for 2.7 miles to the circle for the Windows Trail.

**GPS coordinates:**
38.6872° N, 109.5367° W

**Did you know?**
The North and South Window Arches are often referred to as "The Spectacles" because they look like a pair of glasses when viewed from a distance.

**Journal:**

Date(s) Visited:

Weather
conditions:

Who you were with:

Nature observations:

Special memories:

# Double Arch

This double arch is the tallest and second-longest arch in Arches National Park. It is within the Windows area of the park and a short walk from the Windows Arches. The larger opening is 148 feet wide and 104 feet high.

It is a short half-mile and mostly flat hike along the Double Arch Trail to get to the formation. The arch is unique because it was formed differently from other arches in the park. It is known as a "pothole arch" because the water erosion occurred from above the arch rather than the side.

**Best time to visit:**
Spring or fall

**Pass/Permit/Fees:**
$30 per vehicle, $25 per motorcycle, and $15 per individual. Good for seven days.

**Closest city or town:**
Moab

**How to get there:**
The entrance to the park is five miles north of Moab along Highway 191. Drive 9.2 miles up the Arches Entrance Road/Arches Scenic Drive, then take the first right after Balanced Rock. Continue to follow this road for 2.7 miles until it ends at a circle for the Windows Trail. The Double Arch Trail starts at the far north side of the parking lot.

**GPS coordinates:** 38.6916° N, 109.5403° W

**Did you know?** Double Arch was featured in a scene from the movie *Indiana Jones and the Last Crusade.*

**Journal:**

Date(s) Visited:

Weather conditions:

Who you were with:

Nature observations:

Special memories:

# Devil's Garden Trails

Devil's Garden is on the north side of Arches National Park. In this portion of the park, you'll find arches, spires, narrow rock walls, and breathtaking views. The crown jewel, Landscape Arch, is the longest natural rock span in the world. It sits to the north in Devil's Garden. Its opening is an awe-inspiring 306 feet. The Landscape Arch trail is an easy segment, but the trails get more difficult beyond the arch.

The Double O Arch trail is strenuous, and the alternate route called Primitive Trail is the most difficult segment of the trail system. The entire loop is 7.8 miles. Along with the spectacular views of the area, Devil's Garden also offers activities for every skill level, including camping, backpacking, hiking, and stargazing.

**Best time to visit:**
Spring or fall

**Pass/Permit/Fees:**
$30 per vehicle, $25 per motorcycle, and $15 per individual. Good for seven days.

**Closest city or town:**
Moab

**How to get there:**
The entrance to the park is five miles north of Moab along Highway 191. Follow the main road, Arches Entrance Road/Arches Scenic Drive, all the way to the end. It takes about 30 minutes to reach from the park entrance if you don't stop along the way.

**GPS coordinates:**
38.7829° N, 109.5949° W

**Did you know?**
There is a 150-foot monolith named Dark Angel in Devil's Garden.

**Journal:**

Date(s) Visited:

Weather conditions:

Who you were with:

Nature observations:

Special memories:

# Delicate Arch

Delicate Arch is a massive, red-hued, standalone arch in the eastern part of Arches National Park. With an opening that is 46 feet high and 32 feet wide, it is the largest freestanding arch in the park.

The trail to the arch is three miles roundtrip at a steady incline up to 480 feet. It is rated as moderate. There is also a more easily accessible viewpoint on a lower trail called the Lower Delicate Arch Viewpoint. The less visually obstructed Upper Viewpoint is a short distance away.

**Best time to visit:**
Spring or fall

**Pass/Permit/Fees:**
$30 per vehicle, $25 per motorcycle, and $15 per individual. Good for seven days.

**Closest city or town:**
Moab

**How to get there:**
Trailhead: Drive 11.7 miles north into the park on the main road until you see the righthand turn to Delicate Arch and Wolfe Ranch. Turn right on Delicate Arch Road and drive another 1.2 miles to the parking area on your left.

Viewpoints: Continue past the parking area another 1.2 miles. The road ends at the parking area for the Lower and Upper Delicate Arch viewing areas.

**GPS coordinates:**
38.7436° N, 109.4993° W

**Did you know?**
Delicate Arch has become a widely recognized symbol of the state of Utah and is featured on state license plates.

**Journal:**

Date(s) Visited:

Weather
conditions:

Who you were with:

Nature observations:

Special memories:

# Dead Horse Point State Park

This park features incredible overlooks of the Colorado River and Canyonlands National Park. The scenic vistas of this area are some of the most photographed in the world. The overlook is 2,000 feet above the Colorado River. With eight miles of connected hiking trails that lead to eight different overlooks, there is a lot of canyon country to see.

This location is frequented by mountain bikers. The Intrepid Trail System is an eight-segment mountain biking trail of over 16 miles to ride and enjoy spectacular views. Rated as easy through moderate, many of the bike trails are family-friendly.

The Dead Horse Point State Park is designated as an International Dark Sky Park, and camping is available nearby. Many enjoy that it is one of the few dog-friendly parks.

**Best time to visit:**
Spring or fall

**Pass/Permit/Fees:**
Day use fees, valid for two consecutive days: $20 per vehicle, $10 per motorcycle, and $4 per pedestrian or cyclist.

**Closest city or town:**
Moab

**How to get there:**
Drive nine miles northwest of Moab on US 191, then 23 miles southwest on Utah 313. It is roughly 45 minutes to the visitor center.

**GPS coordinates:**
38.4748° N, 109.7406° W

**Did you know?**
Legend says the park was named Dead Horse because it was used as a natural corral by cowboys long ago, and the horses would sadly often die of exposure.

**Journal:**

Date(s) Visited:

Weather
conditions:

Who you were with:

Nature observations:

Special memories:

# Ken's Lake

Ken's Lake Campground is part of the Ken's Lake Recreation Area. The entire area includes the lake, the campground, a manmade reservoir, a day-use area equipped with a boat ramp, and trails to hike or explore via horseback. Three miles of trails are within the vicinity of the lake. The trails feature views of the Moab Valley and the La Sal Mountains.

The lake is kept stocked with fish, but a Utah fishing license is required if you are over 14 years old. Surrounded by arid desert, Ken's Lake is a perfect place to come and escape the heat. You can swim, fish, and paddle here.

**Best time to visit:**
Any time of year

**Pass/Permit/Fees:**
$20 per campsite per night.

**Closest city or town:**
Moab

**How to get there:**
Drive seven miles south from Moab on Highway 191. Take a left, following signs to Ken's Lake. Continue until you arrive at the lake.

**GPS coordinates:**
38.4815° N, 109.4296° W

**Did you know?**
Ken's Lake is a part of an initiative called the Mills Creek Project that helps provide an irrigation system.

**Journal:**

Date(s) Visited:

Weather
conditions:

Who you were with:

Nature observations:

Special memories:

# Bears Ears National Monument

Bears Ears was designated as a national monument rather recently in 2016. The pair of towering buttes are distinctive against the scenery of the area. The park is divided into two units named Indian Creek and Shash Jaa, and the entire area features expanses of red rock, high plateaus, juniper forests, and a legacy of Native cultures.

You can hike, visit cultural sites, mountain bike, float on the river, and ride off-highway vehicles. Additional activities include scenic drives, camping, wildlife viewing, and paleontological exploration. The land of the monument contains many artifacts and archaeological sites that are historical and sacred. Visitors are urged to learn how to protect the monument before exploring.

**Best time to visit:**
Spring and fall

**Pass/Permit/Fees:**
No entry fee, but some hiking and camping areas have fees— permit required for overnight backpacking at a rate of $8 per person per trip.

**Closest city or town:** Bluff

**How to get there:**
From Bluff, travel north on Highway 191 for 21 miles. Turn left onto UT-95 N and continue 30.2 miles west. Turn right on UT-275 N. After 0.7 miles, turn right onto Elk Mountain/FR008. This 6.1-mile road will take you to the saddle between the two buttes.

**GPS coordinates:**
37.6291611° N, 109.8679093° W

**Did you know?**
Bears Ears was the first national monument ever designated at the request of Indigenous tribes. It's one of the most extensive archaeological areas on Earth.

**Journal:**

Date(s) Visited:

Weather conditions:

Who you were with:

Nature observations:

Special memories:

# *Faux Waterfalls*

It is just a short hike to get to this beautiful desert waterfall. There's even a swimming hole at the base, so bring your swimsuit! The waterfall is very close to Ken's Lake. There are cottonwoods and desert flowers with the scenic cliff as a backdrop.

The drive to the trailhead is somewhat rocky, and a four-wheel-drive vehicle is recommended.

**Best time to visit:**
Any time of year, summer for swimming.

**Pass/Permit/Fees:**
Free

**Closest city or town:**
Moab

**How to get there:**
From Moab, head south on US 191 for about 7.5 miles to mile marker 117.9. Turn left and go east on Ken's Lake Road. Follow for half a mile and turn right onto La Sal Mountain Loop Road. Go south 0.6 miles until the fork in the road, then take the left fork. Follow the road east and turn east onto Ken's Lake Road until you reach Flat Pass Road. The dirt road leads to an unsigned spur road, where you'll turn left and drive half a mile to the trailhead.

**GPS coordinates:**
38.4811° N, 109.4117° W

**Did you know?**
The waterfall is called a faux waterfall because it is a manmade feature using a diversion tunnel from Mill Creek.

**Journal:**

Date(s) Visited:

Weather
conditions:


Who you were with:

Nature observations:


Special memories:

# *Birthing Rock Petroglyphs*

This unique location features ancient rock art. It is a large boulder adorned with petroglyphs on all four sides. Imagery includes a woman giving birth, centipedes, a hunter with a bow, men fighting, and other interesting figures.

The Birthing Rock is one of six sites that comprise the Moab Rock Art Motor Tour along with Moonflower Canyon, Golf Course, Potash Road, Wolf Ranch, and Courthouse Wash.

**Best time to visit:**
Spring and fall

**Pass/Permit/Fees:**
Free

**Closest city or town:**
Moab

**How to get there:**
Take US 191 in Moab to Kane Creek Blvd. Continue south/southwest for 3.8 miles until the road turns into Kane Springs Rd./Moab Kane Creek Blvd. Continue south for 1.4 miles until you see several pullouts to park on your right.

**GPS coordinates:**
38.5219° N, 109.6027° W

**Did you know?**
While it is difficult to determine the exact age of rock art, these petroglyphs are believed to have been created somewhere between 500 and 1540 CE.

**Journal:**

Date(s) Visited:

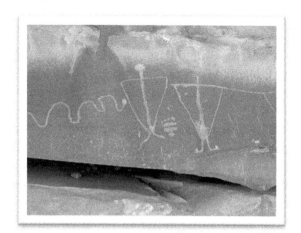

Weather conditions:

Who you were with:

Nature observations:

Special memories:

# Quail Creek State Park

Quail Creek State Park features a great campsite and reservoir within a red rock desert setting. The water is a clear green, surrounded by colorful cliffs and the Pine Valley Mountains.

The 600-acre reservoir is formed by two dams and has a maximum depth of 120 feet. It is cold enough to sustain rainbow trout, bullhead catfish, and crappie, which are all stocked. The warmer, upper levels of water are great for the stocked largemouth bass and bluegill.

The warm waters and mild winter climate make this park a year-round destination. Visitors come to boat, camp, fish, and swim. There are 23 single-family campsites to choose from around the reservoir.

**Best time to visit:**
Any time of year

**Pass/Permit/Fees:**
$15 day-use fee, includes boat ramp use.

**Closest city or town:**
Hurricane

**How to get there:**
From I-15, take the Hurricane exit (exit 16). Travel east on HWY 9, then drive for about three miles toward Hurricane City. Turn left at the second light. The entrance is on the right side of the road.

**GPS coordinates:**
37.1879° N, 113.3941° W

**Did you know?**
The reservoir was completed in 1985 to provide culinary water and irrigation to the nearby St. George area.

**Journal:**

Date(s) Visited:

Weather conditions:

Who you were with:

Nature observations:

Special memories:

# Great Salt Lake & Antelope Island

The largest saltwater lake in the Western Hemisphere, the Great Salt Lake is also the largest lake between the Pacific Ocean and the Great Lakes of the U.S. At 12% salinity, it is saltier than the ocean, so it's easy to float in the water.

Considered to be one of the best ways to enjoy the lake, Antelope Island State Park offers an ideal place to swim and sunbathe along the white sand beaches. You can also kayak and sail. There are full-service marinas available at Antelope Island and the southern shore of the lake. Antelope Islands and Stansbury Island also feature excellent mountain biking trails.

**Best time to visit:**
Fall

**Pass/Permit/Fees:**
$15 per vehicle and $3 per bicycle/motorcycle/pedestrian.

**Closest city or town:**
Salt Lake City

**How to get there:**
The Great Salt Lake is located northwest of Salt Lake City. To Antelope Island: Drive north on I-15 to Syracuse, then west onto SR127. Cross the causeway to Antelope Island. To Great Salt Lake State Park: Go to the south end of the lake along I-80, about 16 miles west of Salt Lake City.

**GPS coordinates:**
41.1158° N, 112.4768° W

**Did you know?**
The average depth of Great Salt Lake is 20 feet, and the maximum depth is 33 feet.

**Journal:**

Date(s) Visited:

Weather
conditions:


Who you were with:

Nature observations:

Special memories:

# *Huntington State Park*

This beautiful setting features crimson buttes coupled with the evergreen colors of pinyon and juniper trees. A quiet desert oasis surrounded by sandstone cliffs and peaks, this scenic place is a perfect spot to come and relax.

The sea-colored, warm water reservoir is great for water skiing, boating, and fishing. The Outback Nature Trail takes you around the reservoir for a 2.7-mile wildlife adventure. There are 25 campsites and numerous picnic sites, so it's suitable for a day or overnight trip.

**Best time to visit:**
Any time of year

**Pass/Permit/Fees:**
$10 day-use fee, including watercraft launches.

**Closest city or town:** Huntington

**How to get there:**
From Salt Lake City, take I-15 south to exit 261 for State Road 6. Continue southeast to exit 241 for State Road 10. Travel 19 miles south on to the park.

**GPS coordinates:**
39.3481° N, 110.9436° W

**Did you know?**
The town and the reservoir were named in honor of the three Huntington Brothers who first explored the area in 1855.

**Journal:**

Date(s) Visited:

Weather conditions:

Who you were with:

Nature observations:

Special memories:

# Red Fleet State Park

In the heart of dinosaur land, Red Fleet State Park provides recreation and a historical experience. Most of the park is dominated by the Red Fleet Reservoir, a 750-acre area that's great for boating, paddleboarding, kayaking, fishing, and swimming. Jumping from the sandstone cliffs surrounding the reservoir is also a popular, albeit dangerous, activity.

There are also numerous hiking and biking trails in the area. Dinosaur tracks have been preserved on the north shores of the reservoir. The area where the tracks are located is called Fossil Trackway. It can be accessed via the Dinosaur Trackway trail. Additionally, there is a campground at the reservoir if you'd like to explore for more than one day. Additional sites like Dinosaur National Monument are nearby, and Red Fleet is an International Dark Sky Park.

**Best time to visit:**
Any time of year

**Pass/Permit/Fees:**
$10 day-use fee

**Closest city or town:**
Vernal

**How to get there:**
Continue on Highway 191 a quarter mile past the entrance road and make a righthand turn onto Donkey Flats road. This is the road that will take you to the Dinosaur Trackway trailhead. Park at the bathrooms and kiosk to enjoy the numerous hiking and biking trails in the area.

**GPS coordinates:**
40.5802° N, 109.4322° W

**Did you know?**
The dinosaur tracks are 200 million years old.

**Journal:**

Date(s) Visited:

Weather conditions:

Who you were with:

Nature observations:

Special memories:

# Sand Hollow State Park

Picture warm blue waters against a red rock landscape and red sand beaches. The reservoir is a great place for water sports, fishing, boating, and swimming. There is also plenty to explore around the shores. The north side is full of slickrock, while the south offers sandy beaches.

One of Utah's newer state parks, Sand Hollow, also features 15,000 acres of pristine sand dunes. There are several off-roading trails so that you can explore the dunes of Sand Mountain. There are even three campgrounds to choose from if you'd rather plan for multi-day adventures. You can drive your ATV from the Sandpit Campground right to the dunes and back for extra fun and convenience.

**Best time to visit:**
May–September

**Pass/Permit/Fees:**
$15 per vehicle. Park entry is included with the camping rate.

**Closest city or town:**
Hurricane

**How to get there:**
From I-15, take the Hurricane exit (exit 16). Travel east on HWY 9 for about four miles to Sand Hollow Road and then turn right. Continue for 4.5 miles, then turn left at the park entrance.

**GPS coordinates:**
37.1200° N, 113.3820° W

**Did you know?**
The reservoir is 1,322 acres, but the entire park occupies 20,000 acres.

**Journal:**

Date(s) Visited:

Weather conditions:

Who you were with:

Nature observations:

Special memories:

# *Starvation Reservoir*

Found inside the Fred Hayes State Park, Starvation Reservoir is secluded and full of natural diversity. The water is a beautiful turquoise, and the reservoir is stocked with fish every season.

There are recreational activities of all kinds, including boating, skiing, paddle boarding, and fishing. You can hike or check out the off-roading trails. There's even an archery course where you can use your own equipment or borrow from the park. There are also developed and primitive campgrounds to stay overnight at this reservoir in the desert.

**Best time to visit:**
May–September

**Pass/Permit/Fees:**
$10 day-use fee

**Closest city or town:**
Duchesne

**How to get there:**
Fred Hayes State Park at Starvation is located four miles northwest of Duchesne on Highway 40.

**GPS coordinates:**
40.1868° N, 110.4674° W

**Did you know?**
There are several different legends tied to the naming of Starvation Reservoir. All of the stories end with starvation caused by the harsh, hostile environment of the late 1800s and early 1900s.

**Journal:**

Date(s) Visited:

Weather conditions:

Who you were with:

Nature observations:

Special memories:

# Glen Canyon Recreation Area

Glen Canyon is a natural canyon that was carved by the Colorado River. Hundreds of miles of scenic vistas and geological wonders can be found in this rugged, high-desert terrain. Glen Canyon Recreation Area encompasses the area around Lake Powell, which lies between the states of Utah and Arizona. It features water-based and backcountry recreation.

Opportunities for fishing, boating, swimming, hiking, kayaking, and four-wheel driving on off-roading trails are available throughout the park. The hike to Horseshoe Bend is one of the most popular day hikes. There are also several routes for scenic drives, such as the Burr Trail and Hole-in-the-Rock Road.

**Best time to visit:**
Fall

**Pass/Permit/Fees:**
$30 per vehicle, $25 per motorcycle, $15 per individual, and $30 per boat/vessel. All are valid for seven days.

**Closest city or town:**
Bullfrog

**How to get there:**
The Bullfrog Visitor Center is located on Utah Highway 276. Ferry Service is provided by the state of Utah from Bullfrog to Halls Crossing. In-park shuttle service is available at Bullfrog.

**GPS coordinates:**
41.3724° N, 112.2026° W

**Did you know?**
Glen Canyon Recreation Area begins at the Grand Canyon in Lees Ferry, AZ, and stretches to the Orange Cliffs of Utah.

**Journal:**

Date(s) Visited:

Weather
conditions:

Who you were with:

Nature observations:

Special memories:

# Rainbow Bridge National Monument

One of the world's largest known natural bridges, Rainbow Bridge National Monument, sees an average of 200,000 to 300,000 visitors per year. Visitors are asked to respect the religious significance of the monument to neighboring tribes and consider viewing the Rainbow Bridge from the viewing area rather than walking up to it.

There are two ways to get to Rainbow Bridge. One option is taking either of the two Navajo Mountain trails, which each take at least two days total, and traverse through canyon country. Both the North Trail and South Trail are over 17 miles and not suitable for a casual hiker. The second way is by boating over Lake Powell to the courtesy boat dock near the observation area. You can take a private vessel or travel on the tour boat. The trail viewing area is approximately one mile.

**Best time to visit:**
Spring or fall

**Pass/Permit/Fees:**
No entrance fee. The permits required for the Navajo Mountain Trail from Navajo Nation Parks & Recreation are $12 per person per day.

**Closest city or town:**
Lake Powell

**How to get there:**
There are no roads in the vicinity. Rainbow Bridge can be reached by boat on Lake Powell or by hiking one of two trails around Navajo Mountain on the Navajo Nation, by permit only. Boat tours are available.

**GPS coordinates:**
37.0683° N, 111.2433° W

**Did you know?**
Rainbow Bridge spans 275 feet and has a height of 290 feet.

**Journal:**

Date(s) Visited:

Weather conditions:

Who you were with:

Nature observations:

Special memories:

# Coral Pink Sand Dunes

The erosion of pink-colored Navajo sandstone from the Middle Jurassic period has created dunes of pink sand. The dunes are estimated to be 10,000–15,000 years old and are surrounded by red sandstone cliffs. The park is at 6,000 feet in elevation.

Of the 3,730 acres, 2,000 acres of sand are open to off-roading adventures. Riders can traverse Sand Highway in a small canyon and the South Boundary Trail. There aren't really any formal trails, and visitors are welcome to explore the dunes on foot, too. The park also allows for camping, photography, and hiking, along with off-roading.

**Best time to visit:**
Spring or fall

**Pass/Permit/Fees:**
$10 per vehicle

**Closest city or town:**
Kanab

**How to get there:**
From Kanab, take Highway 89 north for 10 miles to Hancock Road, which is designated a Scenic Backway. Go seven miles to the intersection with Yellowjacket Road. Turn left (south) onto Yellowjacket. The main park entrance is five miles and to the left.

**GPS coordinates:**
37.0377° N, 112.7144° W

**Did you know?**
Coral Pink Sand Dunes is the only place in the world where the coral pink tiger beetle is found.

**Journal:**

Date(s) Visited:

Weather conditions:

Who you were with:

Nature observations:

Special memories:

# Strawberry Reservoir

Located near the Uinta National Forest of the Watch Mountains, Strawberry Reservoir sits in an open mountain valley. This reservoir is best known for its fishing. As Utah's most popular fishery, more than 1.5 million angling hours are put in at Strawberry Reservoir per year.

There are four major fishing zones in the area, including Strawberry Basin, Meadows Basin, Soldier Creek Basin, and the Narrows. Large rainbow trout, cutthroat trout, and kokanee salmon are a few sought-after catches. There are regulations in place regarding the possession, release, and quantity allowed of certain species of fish.

Aside from fishing, there are also various trails to explore in the area, and camping is available around the reservoir.

**Best time to visit:**
Any time of year. There is even ice fishing.

**Pass/Permit/Fees:**
Non-resident 3-day fishing license: $28. Resident 3-day fishing license: $16. Weekly boat launch pass: $55.

**Closest city or town:**
Fruitland

**How to get there:** From Fruitland, take US 40 W for about 21 miles. Turn left onto Forest Road 131/Strawberry Road. This will take you around the west side of the reservoir, where you can access Strawberry Bay Marina and other picnic areas.

**GPS coordinates:**
40.1718° N, 111.1295° W

**Did you know?**
Currently, the state record for the largest cutthroat trout caught was set at this location in 1930 with a 27-pound fish.

**Journal:**

Date(s) Visited:

Weather
conditions:


Who you were with:

Nature observations:

Special memories:

# Tony Grove Lake

A glacial lake located in the Uinta-Wasatch-Cache National Forest, Tony Grove, has since been augmented by the use of a dam built in the 1930s. Featuring an assortment of summer wildflowers and excellent trails, this location is designated a US Forest Service Wildflower Viewing Area.

There is an easy trail that circles the lake, and there are additional trails that take you into the Mt. Naomi Wilderness or up to White Pike Lake.

Visitors come for fishing, canoeing, paddleboarding, and to enjoy the fresh mountain air. Camping is available at the Tony Grove Lake Campground, which is primitive, and reservations are recommended. There is also primitive wilderness camping in the Mt. Naomi Wilderness area.

**Best time to visit:**
July–August for peak flower viewing.

**Pass/Permit/Fees:**
$6 per car per day, $20 seven-day pass, and $35 full summer pass.

**Closest city or town:**
Logan

**How to get there:**
From Logan, drive northeast on US Highway 89 for 19 miles to the Tony Grove turnoff. From there, drive about seven miles to the end of the road at Tony Grove Lake.

**GPS coordinates:**
41.8927° N, 111.6430° W

**Did you know?**
The name of the lake is derived from its popularity with wealthy residents of Logan in the late 19th and early 20th centuries.

**Journal:**

Date(s) Visited:

Weather conditions:

Who you were with:

Nature observations:

Special memories:

# Fish Lake

At an elevation of 8,848 feet, Fish Lake is a high alpine lake that lies within the Fishlake National Forest. The lake is six miles long and one mile wide. The southeast shore is bonded by the Mytoge Mountains, and the northwest shore is bounded by Fish Lake Hightop Plateau. It is the largest natural mountain lake in the state of Utah. The lake holds large mackinaw, rainbow trout, lake trout, splake, kokanee salmon, brown trout, tiger trout, and yellow perch.

There are several surrounding campgrounds and three boat ramps on the west shore. Multiple trails for hiking and biking can be found in the area as well. The Lakeshore National Recreation Trail is 17 miles long and a great option for exploring by foot or bike. Different sections of the trail offer varying levels of challenge. For a moderate challenge, follow the trail from Bowery Haven Resort up to Pelican Point for a panoramic view of Fish Lake.

**Best time to visit:**
Summer or fall

**Pass/Permit/Fees:**
Camping fees vary by site.

**Closest city or town:**
Koosharem

**How to get there:**
Head north on UT-62 E and turn right onto Browns Lane. Merge onto UT-24 E, then turn left onto UT-25 N.

**GPS coordinates:**
38.5502° N, 111.7078° W

**Did you know?**
The world-famous Pando Aspen Clone is near the lake. It is the world's heaviest living organism at 13 million pounds.

**Journal:**

Date(s) Visited:

Weather conditions:

Who you were with:

Nature observations:

Special memories:

# Mirror Lake

At an elevation of 10,400 feet, Mirror Lake is easily accessed from the Mirror Lake Scenic Byway that brings visitors up into the Uinta Mountains. A popular spot for fishing and recreation, the lake's name comes from the pristine reflection of the surrounding mountains and trees.

You can take a day trip or stay overnight at the Mirror Lake Campground located on the shore of the lake. The lake is surrounded by the Uinta-Wasatch-Cache National Forest, and there is an abundance of trails to explore beyond the lake and into the wilderness.

**Best time to visit:**
August

**Pass/Permit/Fees:**
Day-use fees: $6 for up to three days or $12 for up to seven days. Camping fees vary.

**Closest city or town:**
Kamas

**How to get there:**
From Salt Lake City, take I-80 east for approximately 30 miles to exit 146 for Highway 40 toward Park City/Heber City/Vernal. Take exit 4 onto Highway 248 toward Kamas. Turn left onto UT-32, then right onto Highway 150, the Mirror Lake Scenic Byway. Continue 32 miles to the campground.

**GPS coordinates:**
40.7044° N, 110.8888° W

**Did you know?**
You can enjoy a spectacular view of the lake from atop Bald Mountain. The Mirror Lake Scenic Byway gets you within 1,500 feet of the summit.

**Journal:**

Date(s) Visited:

Weather conditions:

Who you were with:

Nature observations:

Special memories:

# Navajo Lake

Located in the Dixie National Forest, Navajo lake is a small reservoir in Kane County of southern Utah. The lake also has a naturally occurring dam on the eastern side of the valley. The area is host to various lodging facilities, fishing, and boating activities, despite the lake only being about 25 feet deep. Ancient lava beds surround the area, including Mammoth Cave, which can be explored. There are signs that direct travelers to the site. You can also mountain bike a 12-mile loop trail around the lake called the Navajo Lake Loop Trail while catching some great views along the way. There is even a one-mile hiking trail to the nearby Cascade Falls. Camping is available at the Navajo Lake Campground.

**Best time to visit:**
Any time of year

**Pass/Permit/Fees:**
Free to visit. $10 per day for a walk-in tent, $12 per day for a single site, and $20 per day for a double site. Maximum stay permitted is 14 days.

**Closest city or town:**
Cedar City

**How to get there:**
From Cedar City at the intersection of State Routes 130 and 14, take Route 14 east 25.5 miles to Navajo Lake. Follow the signs and turn right, then continue 3.3 miles until you see the campground sign. The
campground is on both sides of the roadway.

**GPS coordinates:**
37.5233° N, 112.7783° W

**Did you know?**
Originally known as Cloud Lake to the Paiutes, Navajo Lake was formed by lava flow many years ago.

**Journal:**

Date(s) Visited:

Weather
conditions:

Who you were with:

Nature observations:

Special memories:

# Other Places

Place:

Date(s) visited:

Weather conditions:

Who you were with:

Nature observations:

Special memories:

Place:

Date(s) visited:

Weather conditions:

Who you were with:

Nature observations:

Special memories:

Place:

Date(s) visited:

Weather conditions:

Who you were with:

Nature observations:

Special memories:

Place:

Date(s) visited:

Weather conditions:

Who you were with:

Nature observations:

Special memories:

Place:

Date(s) visited:

Weather conditions:

Who you were with:

Nature observations:

Special memories:

Place:

Date(s) visited:

Weather conditions:

Who you were with:

Nature observations:

Special memories:

Place:

Date(s) visited:

Weather conditions:

Who you were with:

Nature observations:

Special memories:

Place:

Date(s) visited:

Weather conditions:

Who you were with:

Nature observations:

Special memories:

Place:

Date(s) visited:

Weather conditions:

Who you were with:

Nature observations:

Special memories:

Place:

Date(s) visited:

Weather conditions:

Who you were with:

Nature observations:

Special memories:

# Credit the Incredible Photographers:

Utah Map
https://www.shutterstock.com/image-vector/utah-map-252016582
boreala. (n.d.). Utah Map. Shutterstock. https://www.shutterstock.com/image-vector/utah-map-252016582.

Bear Lake
https://search.creativecommons.org/photos/775d5e90-ca42-4d0d-b604-603a41b9128c
"Bear Lake, Utah Overlook" by Andrew Kalat is licensed with CC BY-ND 2.0. To view a copy of this license, visit https://creativecommons.org/licenses/by-nd/2.0/

Waterfall Canyon
https://search.creativecommons.org/photos/974f2a37-632e-411f-9bc1-6d949cce6292
"Waterfall Canyon 1" by Argyleist is licensed with CC BY 2.0. To view a copy of this license, visit https://creativecommons.org/licenses/by/2.0/

Bonneville Salt Flats
https://search.creativecommons.org/photos/ddcd55d8-13cc-40b8-8bf2-b78f7671e904
"Bonneville Salt Flats" by mypubliclands is licensed with CC BY 2.0. To view a copy of this license, visit https://creativecommons.org/licenses/by/2.0/

Uinta Mountains and Mirror Lake Highway
https://search.creativecommons.org/photos/1c0dadd8-15d6-4f03-83dd-e5e6b7514535
"Hayden Peak over Mirror Lake, High Uinta Mountains, Utah" by Ken Lund is licensed with CC BY-SA 2.0. To view a copy of this license, visit https://creativecommons.org/licenses/by-sa/2.0/

The Canyons near Salt Lake City
https://search.creativecommons.org/photos/ba6f7af4-186c-45dd-9b6b-4acd886e39d3
"Big Cottonwood Canyon, Near Salt Lake City, Utah" by Ken Lund is licensed with CC BY-SA 2.0. To view a copy of this license, visit https://creativecommons.org/licenses/by-sa/2.0/

Bryce Canyon National Park
https://search.creativecommons.org/photos/c6c84363-ca20-4d28-805c-b8e6661a4fe1
"Bryce Canyon National Park," by Bernard Spragg is marked under CC0 1.0. To view the terms, visit https://creativecommons.org/licenses/cc0/1.0/

Flaming Gorge Reservoir
https://search.creativecommons.org/photos/53277727-892f-4712-8d84-9c6b77b4d52a
"Flaming Gorge Reservoir" by a4gpa is licensed with CC BY-SA 2.0. To view a copy of this license, visit https://creativecommons.org/licenses/by-sa/2.0/

Calf Creek Falls
https://search.creativecommons.org/photos/e6415555-e941-44c0-8da3-6aa17a871b47
"Calf Creek Falls right before the crowds showed up" by Alaskan Dude is licensed with CC BY 2.0. To view a copy of this license, visit https://creativecommons.org/licenses/by/2.0/

Mystic Hot Springs
https://search.creativecommons.org/photos/2975fe57-b0b2-4f26-b581-4a7d2ab00216

"Day 2: Yant Flat" by snowpeak is licensed with CC BY 2.0. To view a copy of this license, visit https://creativecommons.org/licenses/by/2.0/

Snow Canyon State Park
https://search.creativecommons.org/photos/8a24f0ae-2f5c-44bf-a495-ac510d078fdf
"Snow Canyon State Park, Near St. George, Utah" by Ken Lund is licensed with CC BY-SA 2.0. To view a copy of this license, visit https://creativecommons.org/licenses/by-sa/2.0/

Canyonlands National Park
https://search.creativecommons.org/photos/ee282c1c-479d-45fa-9cb0-1508fd51b610
"Upheaval Dome, Canyonlands National Park, Utah"by Ken Lund is licensed under CC BY-SA 2.0

Arches National Park
https://search.creativecommons.org/photos/fcc96696-3205-4679-88eb-0857cc8c65fd
"File:Double-O-Arch Arches National Park 2.jpg" by Flicka is licensed with CC BY-SA 3.0. To view a copy of this license, visit https://creativecommons.org/licenses/by-sa/3.0

Zion National Park
https://search.creativecommons.org/photos/530ee8fd-ab9e-40fb-b1f4-d86e8101580b
"Zion National Park" by Wolfgang Staudt is licensed with CC BY 2.0. To view a copy of this license, visit https://creativecommons.org/licenses/by/2.0/

Diamond Fork Hot Springs
https://www.shutterstock.com/image-photo/diamond-fork-hotsprings-early-winter-utah-1261438792
CreekCG. (n.d.). Diamon Fork Hotsprings - Early Winter - Utah. Shutterstock. https://www.shutterstock.com/image-photo/diamond-fork-hotsprings-early-winter-utah-1261438792.

Baker Hot Springs
https://search.creativecommons.org/photos/39a948ce-f610-403e-a470-63b68a02ad3a
"Baker Hot Springs Delta Utah" by A J Cole is licensed with CC BY 2.0. To view a copy of this license, visit https://creativecommons.org/licenses/by/2.0/

Homestead Crater
https://www.atlasobscura.com/places/homestead-crater
Berg, G. (n.d.). Homestead Crater - Midway, Utah - Atlas Obscura. Atlas Obscura. https://www.atlasobscura.com/places/homestead-crater.

Balanced Rock
https://search.creativecommons.org/photos/c1748aa7-8324-421a-b11f-a1ea795241f2
"balanced rock in arches state park utah" by Tim Pearce, Los Gatos is licensed with CC BY 2.0. To view a copy of this license, visit https://creativecommons.org/licenses/by/2.0/

Windows Trail
https://search.creativecommons.org/photos/752fc89e-6fb4-47b3-a105-504ed26a01f8
"Window Arches" by Me in ME is licensed with CC BY 2.0. To view a copy of this license, visit https://creativecommons.org/licenses/by/2.0/

Double Arch
https://search.creativecommons.org/photos/43b65556-f820-4aee-9e46-1f888653b3dd

118

Huntington State Park
https://search.creativecommons.org/photos/7e45e804-fcf6-4a5d-b236-2cdcb3fc3d79
"Collis P. Huntington State Park" by Emily Read is licensed with CC BY-ND 2.0. To view a copy
of this license, visit https://creativecommons.org/licenses/by-nd/2.0/

Red Fleet State Park
https://search.creativecommons.org/photos/fad23ae3-4a10-474a-9800-6a7f4fadada3
"File:Red Fleet State Park in winter.jpg" by Scott Catron from Sandy, Utah, USA is licensed with
CC BY-SA 2.0. To view a copy of this license, visit https://creativecommons.org/licenses/by-
sa/2.0

Sand Hollow State Park
https://search.creativecommons.org/photos/2339ead4-65f8-48dd-9aab-9d85d353d14e
"Sand Hollow State Park" by SassyTowne is licensed with CC BY-ND 2.0. To view a copy of this
license, visit https://creativecommons.org/licenses/by-nd/2.0/

Starvation Reservoir
https://search.creativecommons.org/photos/0d75c669-11a8-4825-8412-52f134275709
"Starvation Reservoir, Duchesne, Utah" by Ken Lund is licensed with CC BY-SA 2.0. To view a
copy of this license, visit https://creativecommons.org/licenses/by-sa/2.0/

Glen Canyon Recreation Area
https://search.creativecommons.org/photos/7035f484-b954-40c0-9000-e22ff60a4c95
"Glen Canyon National Recreation Area" by Bernard Spragg is marked under CC0 1.0. To view
the terms, visit https://creativecommons.org/licenses/cc0/1.0/

Rainbow Bridge National Monument
https://search.creativecommons.org/photos/874436cd-481c-4f10-9f9c-5940e3ee544b
"Rainbow Bridge National Monument Utah." by Bernard Spragg is marked under CC0 1.0. To
view the terms, visit https://creativecommons.org/licenses/cc0/1.0/

Coral Pink Sand Dunes
https://search.creativecommons.org/photos/8f88dc02-26f4-4e0b-a945-8392d62a0148
"Coral Pink Sand Dunes, Kane County, Utah" by Ken Lund is licensed with CC BY-SA 2.0. To
view a copy of this license, visit https://creativecommons.org/licenses/by-sa/2.0/

Strawberry Reservoir
https://search.creativecommons.org/photos/b88a9749-f3fa-4404-9ac2-71dcbb411c2b
"Strawberry Reservoir" by Bureau of Reclamation is licensed with CC BY-SA 2.0. To view a copy
of this license, visit https://creativecommons.org/licenses/by-sa/2.0/

Tony Grove Lake
https://search.creativecommons.org/photos/ca98aeeb-e4bd-40b6-8c0d-bb7c781826d7
"File:TonyGroveLake.JPG" by Kasiarunachalam is licensed with CC BY-SA 3.0. To view a copy of
this license, visit https://creativecommons.org/licenses/by-sa/3.0

Fish Lake
https://search.creativecommons.org/photos/6a9cb8b6-2bb5-4dff-a1a3-9f3e1369c16a
"Fish Lake, Utah" by Ken Lund is licensed with CC BY-SA 2.0. To view a copy of this license, visit
https://creativecommons.org/licenses/by-sa/2.0/

Mirror Lake
https://search.creativecommons.org/photos/1c0dadd8-15d6-4f03-83dd-e5e6b7514535

CPSIA information can be obtained
at www.ICGtesting.com
Printed in the USA
BVHW070019150223
658489BV00010B/303